# Adventure camp

## I like camping

**1** Read. Then write questions using question tags.

|  | Bill | Arthur & Steph |
|---|---|---|
| age | 10 years old | 8 years old |
| nationality | Spanish | Argentinian |
| good at | running | jumping and swimming in the sea |

1 <u>Bill's ten years old, isn't he?</u>

2 _____ ?

3 _____ ?

4 _____ ?

5 _____ ?

6 _____ ?

**2** Order to make sentences.

1 I / hiking / I / like / but/ like/ sailing / don't

_____ .

2 love / diving / I / rock climbing /and

_____ .

3 playing / chess / John / at / is / good

_____ .

4 Emma / fishing / good / but / is / isn't / running / at / she / at / good

_____ .

**3** Read. Then complete.

1 I **like swimming** (✓ swim) in the river, but I _____ (✗ swim) in the sea.

2 She _____ (✓ camp) in the summer but she _____ (✗ camp) in the winter.

3 He _____ (✓ meet) friends but he _____ (✗ help) mum at home.

4 We _____ (✓ run) races but we _____ (✗ play) videogames.

**4** **Look at the pictures. Then write.**

1   Jeff **is good at reading a compass.** _____

2 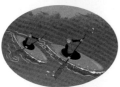  Hilary _____ .

3   They _____ .

4   George _____ .

5   Helen _____ .

6  They _____ .

**5** **Read. Then complete using the present continuous.**

Tom:  What ¹**are you doing**_____ (do), Fran?

Fran:  I ²_____ (pitch) the tent.

Tom:  Where's Sara?

Fran:  I think she ³_____ (light) the campfire. What about you, Tom?

   What ⁴_____ (do)?

Tom:  I ⁵_____ (try) to find my sleeping bag. I put it in my rucksack

   but I can't find it!

Fran:  Jamie ⁶_____ (not do) anything. Why don't you ask him to help you?

Tom:  Good idea. I will! Jamie ...

**6** **Find two questions and the answers. Then write.**

| What | it | rucksack | What | are | singing | they | she |
|------|-----|----------|------|-----|---------|------|-----|
| is | Amy | what | . | Tom | and | is | playing |
| going | doing | ? | tent | are | Janet | sailing | . |
| he | running | She's | big | ? | doing | are | mountains |
| are | pegs | pitching | the | They're | hiking | in | the |

**1** Q: <u>What is</u> _____ ?

**2** A: _____ .

**3** Q: _____ ?

**4** A: _____ .

**7** **Read. Then circle.**

**1** I can read a compass *but / so* I can't light a fire.

**2** It's late *but / so* I'm laying out the bed.

**3** We're hungry *but / so* we are lighting a fire to cook our food.

**4** I'm tired *but / so* I have to take down the tent.

**5** It's dark *but / so* I've got a torch *but / so* I can see.

**6** I'm cold *but / so* I'm lighting a fire.

**7** She likes hiking *but / so* she doesn't like sailing.

**8** **Read. Then complete.**

**1** Your hair looks great! Your sister is a hairdresser, <u>isn't she</u> ?

**2** He likes travelling. He's a tour guide, _____ ?

**3** She helps people when they arrive at the hotel. She's a _____ , _____ ?

**4** He likes plants and flowers. He's a _____ , _____ ?

**5** You work with chemicals. You are a _____ , _____ ?

**6** Your friend is good at singing. He's a _____ , _____ ?

**7** Her cousin is on TV. She's an _____ , _____ ?

**9 Read. Then circle.**

At school we ¹*is / are* doing a project on the rainforest.

² *Before / After* we start, we need to write a plan. I ³ *is work / am working* with Tony and Sarah. We want to find out what people think about deforestation so we ⁴*are writing / is writing* a questionnaire. We ⁵ *is hoping / are hoping* to send the questionnaire to the local government to find out what ⁶ *they are doing / we are doing* about the situation. I love ⁷ *do / doing* project work and our teacher is always ⁸ *finds / finding* us really interesting topics to work on. It's great, ⁹ *is it / isn't it*?

Now I know more about the reasons why deforestation happens. It's sad but some people are more interested in selling trees than conserving our forests!

**10 Read. Then number the sentences in order.**

What projects are you doing at school? ☐

Are you enjoying it? ☐

I don't know but I'm writing a letter to find out what we can do. ☐

Is there anything we can do? ☐

Yes, they're helping me with my homework and looking for new websites. ☐

We're doing a project on protecting animals in the rainforests. ☐

That's great. Bye, Jo! ☐

Yes. I love it. We are studying different monkeys and how we are destroying their homes. ☐

Are your parents helping you? ☐

Hi, Jo! ☐

# Wildlife park

### A rhino is heavier than a turtle

**1** **Write questions. Then find out the answers.**

1  Is a turtle heavier than a rhino? _____  (turtle / heavy / rhino)

   _____ .

2  _____  (camels / tall / monkeys)

   _____ .

3  _____  (cheetah / fast / tiger)

   _____ .

4  _____  (elephant / heavy / whale)

   _____ .

5  _____  (birds / light / butterflies)

   _____ .

**2** **Order to make questions. Then find out the answers.**

1  heavy / baby / elephant / how / a / is

   _____ ?

   **?** _____ .

2  tall / giraffe / is / how / a

   _____ ?

   **?** _____ .

3  long / anaconda / is / an / how

   _____ ?

   **?** _____ .

4  big / Whale / Blue / how/ a / is

   _____ ?

   **?** _____ .

# 2  The cheetah is the fastest animal

**3** **Match. Then write sentences.**

| **1** cheetah | **2** butterfly | **3** elephant | **4** turtle | **5** whale |
|---|---|---|---|---|

| **a** long | **b** fast | **c** heavy | **d** slow | **e** light |
|---|---|---|---|---|

1 [b]  The cheetah is the fastest animal.

2 [ ]  _____ .

3 [ ]  _____ .

4 [ ]  _____ .

5 [ ]  _____ .

**4** **Order to make questions. Then answer for yourself.**

1 tallest / who / your / class / is / the / child / in

_____ ?

_____ .

2 longest / hair / your / class / who / got / has / the / in

_____ ?

_____ .

3 biggest / the / building / your / town / where / is / in

_____ ?

_____ .

4 most / statue / which / is / your / in / the / important / town

_____ ?

_____ .

5 in / are / the / you / your / shortest / class / child

_____ ?

_____ .

**5** **Read. Then complete using the passive.**

### Animal Rescue

Many animals ¹ __are rescued__ (rescue) every day. They ² _____

(help) by people who work to protect the environment. Some of these animals

³ _____ (take) to zoos. In the zoos, the animals ⁴_____

(look after) by vets and other people who work with animals. Today, many

animals ⁵_____ (protect) but there are still a lot of people who

don't respect these rules. What can we do?

**6** **Read. Then rewrite using the passive.**

**A strange story**

I see an elephant walking down the High Street in our town!
The baker catches it and takes it to the police station.
A police officer calls a vet. The vet comes and takes the elephant back to the zoo.

**A strange story**

An elephant ¹_____ (see) walking down the High Street in our town!

It ²_____ (catch) and ³_____ (take) to the police station.

A vet ⁴_____ (call) by a police officer and the elephant

⁵_____ (return) to the zoo.

**7** **Read. Then complete.**

1 Swans can __be found__ (find) on lakes and rivers.

2 Octopus can _____ (see) in the sea or at the aquarium.

3 A lot of information can _____ (find) from fossils.

4 We know about dinosaurs because their fossils _____ (study) by palaeontologists.

5 Fish _____ (eat) by otters.

6 Animals _____ (look after) in wildlife parks.

**8** **Read. Then circle.**

### The Serengeti National Park

Have you ever been to the Serengeti National Park in Africa? It's one of
[1] *the biggest* / *bigger than* and [2] *most famous* / *more famous than* national
parks in Africa and [3] *larger than* / *the largest* in Tanzania. It is one of
[4] *the oldest* / *older than* places on the planet.

It also has [5] *the biggest* / *bigger than* movement of animals in the world called
'migration'. Every year millions of animals move from one place to another at
the same time. Of course, some animals are [6] *slower than* / *the slowest* others
but they all get there in the end.

Some of the best-known animals in the park are the lions, elephants, cheetahs,
giraffes and crocodiles. They are [7] *looked after* / *look after* by Park Rangers.
Although the animals in the SNP [8] *are protected* / *are protect*, sometimes they
[9] *hunt* / *are hunted* by people who want their skins or their teeth. Last year
a lot of elephants [10] *died* / *die* for this reason.

The best time to go is in February and March, shortly just [11] *before* / *after* the
baby animals have been born, but [12] *before* / *after* the big migration.

**9** **Order to make sentences.**

1 fox / more / a / weasel / a / is / intelligent / than

_____ .

2 are / the / playful / monkeys / animals / most

_____ .

3 palaeontologists / by / fossils / studied / are

_____ .

4 is / heaviest / the / in / world / blue / whale / the / animal / the

_____ .

5 animals / sometimes / jungle / in / new / are / discovered / the

_____ .

6 longer / worms / are / snakes / than

_____ .

# Where we live

### It's next to the cinema

**1** **Read. Then complete the map with the places in colour.**

**1** The chemist is next to the college.

**2** On the corner of Charing Cross Road and Coronation Street, opposite the chemist, is the factory.

**3** In between the shopping centre and the factory is the theatre.

**4** The cinema is opposite the theatre, on Coronation Street.

**5** The newsagent in on the corner of Portobello Road and Coronation Street opposite the shopping centre.

**6** The post office is in Coronation Street opposite the restaurant and next to the shopping centre.

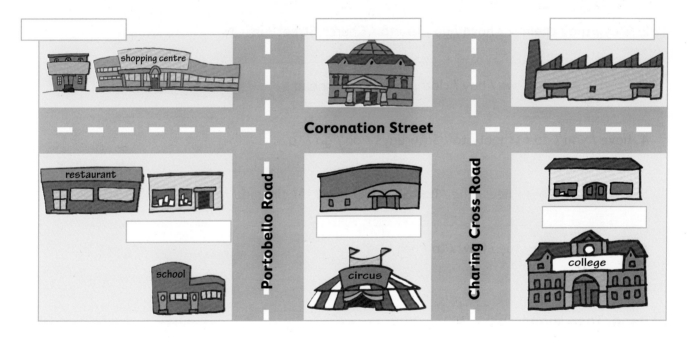

**2** **Look at the map in Activity 1. Then complete.**

| straight ahead | next to | turn right (x2) | opposite |
| --- | --- | --- | --- |

**Tom:** How do you get to the college?

**Sam:** Well, we're at the school now, so you go [1]_____ then

[2]_____ at the corner of Portobello Road and Coronation Street.

Then [3]_____ onto Charing Cross Road.

The college is [4]_____ the chemist and [5]_____ the circus.

# 3 If you turn left, you'll see it

**3** **Read. Then match.**

1  Turn left at the corner

2  I have to finish my homework

3  If I have time,

4  How do I get to the cinema?

5  If she wants to pass the test,

6  If you go to the library,

a  she'll have to study.

b  Go straight ahead and it's on your left!

c  because we have a test tomorrow.

d  and then go straight ahead.

e  you'll find many books.

f  I'll go to the cinema.

**4** **Reorder to make sentences.**

1  she / to / go / the / bookshop / wants / to / new

_____.

2  they / the / chemist / have / go / to / to / Church Street / in

_____.

3  to / some / new / we / buy / clothes / summer / need

_____.

4  have / you / do / school / to / Saturdays / on / go / to

_____?

5  Tom / see / goes / new / the / Batman / to / film / if / cinema / he'll / the

_____.

6  post office / do / the / how / to / get / I

_____?

**5** **Read. Then complete.**

1  If you ___**want to go**___ (want / go) swimming you will ___**have to take**___ (have / take)
   your swimsuit.

2  If you _____ (want / buy) a newspaper you will _____ (have / go)
   to the newsagent.

3  If you _____ (want / see) the film you will _____ (have / buy) a
   cinema ticket.

4  If you _____ (want / have fun) you will _____ (should /go) to the circus.

5  If you _____ (want / pass) your test, you _____ (should /study).

6  If you _____ (want / walk), you _____ (should /go) to the park.

**6** **Read. Then write sentences using *used to* and *didn't use to*.**

| Sara | hair | clothes | home |
|---|---|---|---|
| when she was little | long | dresses | small town |
| now | short | jeans | big city |

1  Sara used to have long hair.

   Now she _____

2  _____ .

   _____ .

3  _____ .

   _____ .

**7** **Find and write three questions. Then answer for yourself.**

| What | what | think | to | do | at | we | use | didn't |
|---|---|---|---|---|---|---|---|---|
| did | you | go | use | you | the | weekends | ? | go |
| I | use | see | What | did | had | did | Where | they |
| do | to | younger | ? | used | use | you | used | ? |
| when | you | were | visit | do | to | go | on | holiday |

1  Q: What did _____ ?

   A: _____ .

2  Q: _____ ?

   A: _____ .

3  Q: _____ ?

   A: _____ .

**8** **Read. Then write sentences using *used to*.**

1  When my mum was younger she _____

   _____ .

2  When my grandad was younger he _____

   _____ .

3  When my dad was younger he _____

   _____ .

## 9 Read. Then match.

1 If I wear my coat,

2 If we go to Greece,

3 If it's sunny,

4 If I take a lot of books with me,

5 If you want to find the theatre,

a we'll learn about a different culture.

b I won't get wet.

c I can read all day every day!

d you'll have to turn right and go east.

e we'll go to the beach.

## 10 Read. Then circle.

1 If it's sunny after school, *I'll / I go* to the beach.

2 If I *will get / get* home early, I'll play on my computer.

3 If he *is / will be* lucky, he'll spend his birthday at the football stadium!

4 If it rains, *they'll / they* go to the cinema.

5 What will you do if you *are / will be* late for school?

6 We'll move to the city if mum *will get / gets* a new job.

## 11 What about you? Write sentences using *used to* and *didn't use to*.

1 _____ .

2 _____ .

3 _____ .

4 _____ .

5 _____ .

6 _____ .

## 12 How do you get from school to your home? Write.

_____

_____

_____

_____

# Good and bad days

### Yesterday I watched a DVD

**1** **Order to make sentences.**

**1** yesterday / I / family / watched / DVD / a / my / with

_____ .

**2** couldn't / because / he / have / he / plate / dropped / dinner / the

_____ .

**3** Saturday / because / was / it / I / bed / to / late / went

_____ .

**4** cooked / mother / last / her / paella / Saturday

_____ .

**2** **Read. Then match.**

**1** Yesterday afternoon I played          **a** to school by bus.

**2** Last night I watched          **b** a really great film.

**3** Last month I sang          **c** my birthday.

**4** This morning I went          **d** in a tennis match.

**5** Two days ago it was          **e** in a school concert.

**3** **What did you do last weekend? Write sentences about yourself.**

| be | give | fall | play | bring | have | get up |

_I got up at_ _____ .

_____ .

_____ .

_____ .

_____ .

**4** **Read. Then write the opposite.**

1 I was late because I missed the bus.

___I wasn't late because I didn't miss the bus.___

2 I didn't play football because it was raining.

_____ .

3 We didn't miss the swimming competition because we arrived on time.

_____ .

4 We went to the beach because we were on holiday.

_____ .

5 We didn't go outside because it was raining.

_____ .

**5** **Read. Then write correctly.**

1 Yesterday it <u>weren't</u> raining so I <u>decide</u> to go to school by bike.

___Yesterday it wasn't raining so___ _____ .

2 It take me forty minutes. I were very tired when I got to school!

_____ .

3 We have Maths first lesson and I fall asleep!

_____ .

4 The teacher didn't said anything until the end of the lesson.

_____ .

5 The bell rings and I wake up. My teacher is looking at me!

_____ .

**6** **Read. Then match.**

1 I dropped the ball and we lost the game.          a  It made me tired!

2 I passed the final exam.                           b  It made me proud!

3 My mum made a chocolate cake for my birthday.     c  It made me angry!

4 I ran races all day in my school sports day.       d  It made me happy!

**7 Read. Then circle.**

Yesterday afternoon I [1] *were / was* watching a film on TV with my brother. It [2] *was / were* very funny and we [3] *was / were* laughing a lot! My parents [4] *was / were* in the garden. They [5] *were / was* planting tomatoes. My sister [6] *were / was* cooking cheese omelettes and dumplings for us in the kitchen and my grandparents [7] *were / was* reading the newspaper in the living room. The cat *was / were* sleeping on the sofa.

**8 Look at the pictures. Then answer.**

1 What was he doing this morning?

_____

2 What were her sisters doing last night before dinner?

_____

3 What was his family doing last weekend?

_____

4 What was her best friend doing yesterday afternoon?

_____

**9** **Read. Then complete.**

Yesterday the weather ¹ __was__ (be) warm and sunny so my parents ² _____ (decide)

to have a picnic on the beach. I ³ _____ (invite) two of my best friends and we

⁴ _____ (spend) the day eating, drinking and playing volleyball on the beach.

Mum and dad ⁵ _____ (prepare) all the food. I ⁶ _____ (get) all the knives

and forks ready. My friends ⁷ _____ (bring) the volleyball and the net, which we

⁸ _____ (put up) in the sand. When we ⁹ _____ (stop) playing

volleyball, we ¹⁰ _____ (swim) in the sea to cool off! It ¹¹ _____

(be) just fantastic. We ¹² _____ (not want) to go home!


**10** **Order to make questions. Then answer for yourself.**

**1** you / last / doing / night / what / were

_____ ?

_____ .

**2** breakfast / what / you / for / did / have

_____ ?

_____ .

**3** holiday / where / you / last / did / go / on / year

_____ ?

_____ .

**4** 10:00 / watching/ at / you / were / TV / night / last

_____ ?

_____ .

**5** Maths / you / did / last / study / night

_____ ?

_____ .

**6** you / sushi / last / eat / weekend / did

_____ ?

_____ .

# Arts and entertainment 5

## You did it by yourself, didn't you?

**1 Read. Then match.**

1 You did the homework by yourself,

2 You were at home last night,

3 Your parents have got a new car,

4 She has got a lot of friends,

5 You can sing well,

6 It was Friday yesterday,

7 They went to the cinema last night,

8 You didn't pass your test,

a hasn't she?

b can't you?

c didn't you?

d did you?

e didn't they?

f haven't they?

g wasn't it?

h weren't you?

**2 Read. Then complete and answer.**

1 You haven't listened to the CD, __have you?__  __No, I haven't.__ (✗)

2 Your best friend, Harry, can't run very fast, _____? _____ (✔)

3 We haven't got a test today, _____? _____ (✗)

4 Your friends didn't go to the party, _____? _____ (✗)

5 You were late for school, _____? _____ (✔)

6 You are very intelligent, _____? _____ ! (✔)

7 If you turn right you'll find the library, _____? _____ (✔)

**3 Read. Then complete.**

1 When you were younger you didn't like watching thrillers by __yourself,__ __did you?__

2 She cooked rice and beans by _____ , _____ ?

3 Last weekend they wrote a cartoon story by _____ , _____ ?

4 Last summer we went on the underground by _____ , _____ ?

5 Yesterday afternoon you went to the swimming pool by _____ , _____ ?

6 They didn't learn to play the drums by _____ , _____ ?

7 Your mum prepared a delicious paella by _____ , _____ ?

## 5 Have you ever seen an alien?

**4** **Read and complete the questions. Then answer for yourself.**

1 How long have you _____ (know) your best friend?

_____ .

2 How long have you _____ (study) English?

_____ .

3 Have you ever _____ (ride) a camel?

_____ .

4 Have you ever _____ (play) the drums?

_____ .

5 How long have you _____ (be) at school?

_____ .

6 Have you _____ (win) a competition recently?

_____ .

**5** **Look at Tom's list. Then write sentences.**

1 <u>He's practised the guitar.</u>

2 _____ .

3 _____ .

4 _____ .

5 _____ .

6 _____ .

To do:
✔ practise guitar
  do homework
✔ call Emma
✔ finish story
  put clothes in wardrobe
  tidy room

**6** **What have you done today? What haven't you done yet? Write your list.**

_____

_____

_____

_____

_____

**7 Read. Then circle.**

1 They *sang / were singing* karaoke when the music *stopped / was stopped*.

2 The audience *were talking / talked* when the film *beginning / began*.

3 We *had / were having* lunch when a dog *was running / ran* into the school dining room.

4 We *packed / were packing* our bags when the taxi *arrived / was arriving*.

5 I *was doing / did* my homework when the teacher *came / was coming* into class.

6 I *was having / had* a shower when my mum *call / called* me.

**8 Order to make sentences.**

1

going / cinema / the / to / I / me/ when / you / saw / was

_____ .

2

surfing / web / the / was / arrived / friend / my / I / when

_____ .

3

visiting / theatre/ heard / news / the / we / we / when / were /the

_____ .

4

apple / an / eating / I / was / a / I / found / when / worm

_____ .

5

me / called / was / I / country / listening / when / to / music / you

_____ .

**9  Look at the table. Then write sentences.**

|  | John | Emma |
|---|---|---|
| study / German | 2 years | 5 years |
| live / Spain | 12 years | 10 years |
| know / Tom | 1 year | 2 years |

1  <u>John has studied German for two years.</u>

2  _____ .

3  _____ .

4  _____ .

5  _____ .

6  _____ .

**10  Read. Then complete.**

does   does   have   for   already   do   was   don't   have   hasn't   haven't   when

Tom doesn't play the guitar, ¹_____ he?

Yes, he ²_____ . He ³_____ practised for a few weeks but he's ⁴_____ passed his first guitar exam.

Wow! You don't play, ⁵_____ you?

No, I ⁶_____ . I play the piano.

How long ⁷_____ you played the piano?

I've had lessons ⁸_____ a long time – 8 years! ⁹_____ you ever tried playing a musical instrument.

No, I ¹⁰_____ . But I ¹¹_____ watching TV last night ¹²_____ I heard this amazing guitarist and now I want to try!

## First, I'll go to the museum

**1 Read. Then order the conversation.**

First, I'll go to the museum ☐

Yes, I hope so. ☐

You will see the big tower inside the castle! ☐

Then, I'll go to the castle ☐

What will you do tomorrow? ☐

No, never. I can't wait to see how big it is! ☐

That's really cool! Have you ever been on the big wheel? ☐

And finally I'll go to the amusement park ☐

**2 Read. Then write about Sara.**

|  | Tomorrow | |
|---|---|---|
|  | Tom | Sara |
| visit palace | ✔ | ✔ |
| go to amusement park | ✔ | (✔) |
| go on dodgems | ✗ | ✔ |
| play mini golf | (✔) | ✗ |

Tomorrow Tom thinks he'll visit the palace first.

Then he'll go to the amusement park.

Later he won't go on the dodgems but he would like to play mini golf.

**Tomorrow Sara thinks** _____

_____

_____

_____

**3 What will you do this weekend? Write.**

First, _____ .

Then, _____ .

Last, _____ .

# 6  What shall we do today?

**4** **Find the conversation. Then complete.**

| What | do | this | afternoon | swimming | ? | that's | Yes |
|---|---|---|---|---|---|---|---|
| shall | we | when | ? | go | The | perfect | . |
|  | they | will | Shall | we | sea | . | boats |
| this | Okay | . | warm | be | will | then | the |
| do | . | What | else | ? | Let's | go | on |

What shall we ¹_____
_____ ?

² _____ swimming?
The ³ _____ .

Okay. ⁴ _____ ?

Let's ⁵ _____ .

⁶ _____ .

**5** **Read. Then complete using *shall* or *could*.**

**Rob:**  I'm bored. ¹_____**Shall**_____ we go to the water park?

**Sam:**  I'm bored, too. Yes, let's go to the water park. ²_____ we go on the boating lake?

**Rob:**  I haven't been there before. Have you?

**Sam:**  Yes. It's great fun. I ³_____ teach you how to row the boat. It's very easy.

**Rob:**  Oh, yes. Then we ⁴_____ have a race to the other side of the lake.

**Sam:**  I think we have to wear life jackets. The lake is quite deep in the middle.

**Rob:**  Yes. Good idea. I ⁵_____ ask Bill where to get them from.

**Sam:**  Okay. Let's go!

**6** **Read. Then complete the table.**

> **The weather.**
> This morning will start off sunny with some clouds in the South. There will be some wind but it won't be very strong. In the North it'll be cloudy and it might rain. The wind will get stronger by this evening. Tomorrow will be sunny all over the country with high temperatures, more than 24°C, except in the North where there will be some strong winds and it may rain in the afternoon. The rest of the week will stay sunny and warm with some wind in the North.

| Today | wind | sun | cloud | dry |
|---|---|---|---|---|
| North | ✔ | | | |
| South | | | | |

**Tomorrow**

| | wind | sun | cloud | dry |
|---|---|---|---|---|
| North | | | | |
| South | | | | |

**Rest of week**

| | wind | sun | cloud | dry |
|---|---|---|---|---|
| North | | | | |
| South | | | | |

**7** **Read the table again. Then write questions and answers.**

1 <u>Will it rain in the South tomorrow?</u>　(✗) <u>No, it won't.</u>　(rain/South/tomorrow)

2 _____ ? (✔) _____ (windy/North/today)

3 _____ ? (✗) _____ (cold/South/tomorrow)

4 _____ ? (✔) _____ (rain/North/tomorrow)

5 _____ ? (✔) _____ (sunny/rest of week)

**8** **Order to make sentences.**

1 sunny / may / go / we / it's / if / lake /boating / the / on

_____ .

2 rains / might / to / go / museum / the / we / if / it

_____ .

3 try / play / your / saxophone / I / to / may

_____ ?

4 jazz / might / go / a / concert / to / with / dad / my / I

_____

**9** **Read Jill's diary. Then answer.**

> It'll be the last day of my holiday tomorrow. The weather will be good so I'll spend the day out in the mountains with my family. We will have time to climb the highest mountain. We haven't climbed that yet. I will have to wear my hiking boots. It will take about five hours to climb the mountain. I might pack my bags in the evening when we get back, but I might leave it until the morning! We'll have lots of time.
>
> What else do I need to do before we go? I'll have to look online to check the plane will be on time. And I'll need to get a few more presents to take home for my friends and family. I hope they'll fit into my bag! I could ask my Mum to put something in her bag if there's not enough space in mine! Okay. I'm going for a swim now. I'll sort everything else out later!

**1** What will Jill do tomorrow?

<u>She will spend the day out in the mountains with her family.</u>

**2** Why?

_____ .

**3** Will she wear her hiking boots?

_____ .

**4** How long will it take to climb the mountain?

_____ .

**5** What will she do in the evening?

_____ .

**6** What else will she do before leaving?

_____ .

**7** What will she do with any extra presents?

_____ .

**8** Will she sort out everything before her swim?

_____ .

## You should read more books

**1** **Order to make sentences.**

**1** do / sport / I / to / ought / more

_____ .

**2** interesting / I / books / more / should / read

_____ .

**3** the / stars / I / looking / at / go / to / had/ better / stop / bed / and

_____ .

**4** telescope / for/ should / a / get / you / look / to / comets

_____ .

**2** **Read. Then match.**

**1** My mum ought to be an astronaut.          **a** You can see dolphins there!

**2** I'd better find my book.          **b** I haven't finished it yet.

**3** My class should visit the aquarium.          **c** It's getting late.

**4** We ought to get up.          **d** She loves looking at the stars.

A

B

C

D

**3** **Read and find the mistakes. Then write correctly.**

**1** I ought visit my granny next week.

_____ .

**2** I should leaving now to catch the bus.

_____ .

**3** I would had better save my pocket money if I want to buy a telescope.

_____ .

# The red planet is the most interesting

**4 Read. Then write the opposite.**

1 Mount Everest is the lowest mountain in the world.

**No, it isn't! It's the highest mountain!**

2 The River Nile is the shortest river in the world.

No, it isn't! _____ .

3 Jupiter is the smallest planet in the solar system.

_____ .

4 Antarctica is the hottest place in the world.

_____ .

**5 Write sentences. Do you agree? Write ✔ or ✗.**

Films:

1 **Batman 3 is more frightening than Batman 1 and Batman 2.** ☐

**It's the most frightening film.**

(Batman 3 / Batman 1 / Batman 2 – frightening)

2 Books: ☐

_____ .

_____ .

(Harry Potter 7 / Harry Potter 5 / Harry Potter 6 – interesting)

3 School subjects: ☐

_____ .

_____ .

(Maths / English / History – complicated)

4 Space technology: ☐

_____ .

_____ .

(space station / rocket / telescope – expensive)

5 Planets: ☐

_____ .

_____ .

(Mars / Neptune / Jupiter – amazing)

**6** **Read the conversation between Jo and Dan. Then complete what Jo tells Sam.**

**Dan:** The stars tonight are amazing!

**Jo:** But it's cloudy....

**Dan:** No. The sky is really clear. And there's no moon.

**Jo:** It's cloudy over my house!

**Dan:** I've just got out of bed. I'm in my garden.

**Jo:** You're mad!

**Dan:** I'm in my pyjamas!

**Jo:** Really mad!

**Dan:** No. Really. The stars look bigger than other days.

...

**Jo:** Hi Sam! I've just spoken to Dan.

**Sam:** Is he OK?

**Jo:** I don't know! I think he's going a bit crazy! He says that ¹ __the stars are amazing__ .

He says that the sky ² _____ and that ³ _____ .

He just ⁴ _____ bed .

**Sam:** Where is he now?

**Jo:** He ⁵ _____ that he's in ⁶ _____ and

that ⁷ _____ his pyjamas!

**Sam:** Oh dear! Too much star-watching I think!

**7** **Transform into a dialogue between Charlotte and Sophie.**

Charlotte says she wants to be an astronaut. Her cousin Sophie says that could be very frightening. Charlotte says that it would be very interesting and not frightening but Sophie says that she might meet horrible aliens! Charlotte says she wants to buy a telescope to look at the planets and Sophie says that it's very expensive.

**Charlotte:** ¹ __I want to be an astronaut.__

**Sophie:** ² _____

**Charlotte:** ³ _____

**Sophie:** ⁴ _____

**Charlotte:** ⁵ _____

**Sophie:** ⁶ _____

**8 Read. Then circle.**

To: dansimpson@homemail.com

Subject: Shooting stars!

**Hi Dan.**

You ¹ *should / have to* look at the stars! They're amazing! They're much bigger than usual. And, tonight ² *is / was* the best night to see shooting stars. I've already seen eleven. They come from every direction so you need to keep looking! You ³ *had to / have to* be quick though. I think ⁴ *it'll / it won't* be cloudy later and ⁵ *we'll / we won't* be able to see anything. My teacher said that it will ⁶ *being / be* one of the best shows of shooting stars for years. Do you think your parents will let you go to bed late? I hope so! Doesn't your dad teach Astronomy at the university? Perhaps he'll let you use his new telescope ⁷ *latest / later*? Or is it ⁸ *most complicated / more complicated than* his old one? If you can, you ⁹ *had better / should*. It will be fantastic. ¹⁰ *You'd / You've* better send me any images you get! Okay? ¹¹ *I'd / I've* better go now. Chat later.

Jamie

**9 Read. Then match.**

1 Hi Jamie. The stars are the

2 My dad said I could

3 He said I had better

4 He'll

5 I'd better

6 This will

a see them if you can come to my house.

b be exciting!

c put my winter coat on because it's cold outside.

d take some photos and you can see them online.

e give me a quick lesson!

f best I've ever seen.

**10 Read. Then write.**

1 I'm taller than my sister.    He says that _____ .

2 She likes travelling.    She says that _____ .

3 The moon is amazing tonight.    They say that _____ .

4 We went to see our granny.    They say that _____ .

# The environment 8

## We're going to plant trees

**1 Read. Then complete.**

|  | Monday | Tuesday | Wednesday | Thursday | Friday |
|---|---|---|---|---|---|
| **Paula** | plant trees | pick up rubbish in the playground | reuse plastic bags | turn off the lights after class | take the bottles to the bottle bank |
| **Jamie** | pick up rubbish in the playground | put paper in the recycling box | turn off the lights after class | plant trees | reuse plastic bags |
| **Ben** | turn off the lights after class | put paper in the recycling box | plant trees | pick up rubbish in the playground | reuse plastic bags |
| **Sue** | take the bottles to the bottle bank | turn off the lights after class | reuse plastic bags | put paper in the recycling box | pick up rubbish in the playground |

1 <u>Sue is going to</u> _____ . (Sue / Monday)

2 _____ . (Ben / Tuesday)

3 _____ . (Sue / Friday)

4 _____ . (Jamie and Ben / Friday)

5 _____ . (Paula / Thursday)

**2 Read the table in Activity 1. Then answer.**

1 Is Ben going to plant trees on Monday?

   <u>**No, he isn't. He's going to turn off the lights after class.**</u>

2 Is Sue going to pick up rubbish in the playground on Wednesday?

   _____ .

3 Are Jamie and Ben going to reuse plastic bags on Tuesday?

   _____ .

4 Is Paula going to turn off the lights after class on Friday?

   _____ .

5 Is Ben going to put paper in the recycling box on Thursday?

   _____ .

## 3 Write questions. Then answer.

**1** he / collect / rubbish/ street

**Is he going to collect rubbish from the street?**    ✗  **No, he isn't.**

**2** they / protect / environment

_____ ?  ✔ _____

**3** we / plant / tree/ school

_____ ?  ✔ _____

**4** mum / reuse / plastic bags / supermarket

_____ ?  ✗ _____

**5** you / use / less water / do the washing up

_____ ?  ✔ _____

**6** your sister / stop / have / baths

_____ ?  ✗ _____

## 4 Read. Then match.

| | | |
|---|---|---|
| **1** I'm going to recycle paper | | **a** it was my turn to go. |
| **2** I've got a cold | | **b** it's my birthday. |
| **3** I didn't pass my test | | **c** it'll be faster. |
| **4** I went to the bottle bank | because | **d** I didn't put a jumper on. |
| **5** I'm having a sleepover | | **e** I didn't revise. |
| **6** We're going by train | | **f** it helps to save trees. |

## 5 Look at the pictures. What are they going to do? Write sentences.

**1** **She is going to recycle paper.** _____

**2** _____

**3** _____

**4** _____

**5** _____

**6** _____

**6** **Order to make sentences.**

1 good / weather / if / is / camping / we'll / go / the

_____ .

2 later / to / do / nothing / we / if / the / go / we'll / cinema / have / to

_____ .

3 soon / if / train / the / we'll / leave / miss / don't / we

_____ .

4 don't / I / won't / the / harder / win / if / competition / practise / I

_____ .

5 pass / study / more / to / have / want / you / if / exam / your / to / you'll

_____ .

**7** **Read. Then complete using** _will_**.**

1 What __will you do__ (_you / do_) if ___you get___ (_you / get_) lots of money for your birthday?

2 If _____ (_you / paint_) a picture, who _____ (_you / give_) it to?

3 If _____ (_you / finish_) the exercise early, _____ (_you / tell_) the teacher?

4 If _____ (_you / have_) a lot of homework today, when _____ (_you / do_) it?

5 Who _____ (_you / tell_) first if _____ (_you / get_) 100% in your test?

6 Where _____ (_you / go_) for the summer if the weather _____ (_be_) hot?

**8** **Read the questions in Activity 7. Then answer for yourself.**

1 _If I get lots of money for my birthday, I'll spend it all in the shopping centre!_

2 _____ .

3 _____ .

4 _____ .

5 _____ .

6 _____ .

**9** **Read. Then complete using *going to, would, because, will*.**

Next weekend, my scouts group is ¹ __**going to clean up**__ (clean up) an old house.

We ² _____ (use) it as an information centre to tell people about

protecting our environment. We ³ _____ (like) to have information

about different ways people can help to look after our environment. For example, we

could ask them to help us to build a bottle bank and a paper recycling centre.

It ⁴ _____ (take) quite a long time but when it's finished, it

⁵ _____ (make) a big difference. And, if it works, we

⁶ _____ (recycle) rubbish, and we'll be able to conserve energy

⁷ _____ everyone is helping. I really hope our community gets involved.

**10** **What are you going to protect the environment? Write five sentences.**

| Five things I'm going to do to protect the environment |
|---|
| **1** |
| **2** |
| **3** |
| **4** |
| **5** |

**11** **Read. Then match.**

**1** If you go to China

**2** If you go to the countryside and smell the flowers

**3** If you are allergic

**4** If you have a severe allergic reaction

**a** you may start sneezing.

**b** you should call an ambulance.

**c** you may see people wearing special masks.

**d** you may have red eyes.